George Weiser

Nine Months in Rebel Prisons

George Weiser

Nine Months in Rebel Prisons

ISBN/EAN: 9783744794701

Printed in Europe, USA, Canada, Australia, Japan

Cover: Foto ©Thomas Meinert / pixelio.de

More available books at **www.hansebooks.com**

NINE MONTHS

IN

Rebel Prisons,

BY

GEORGE WEISER,

Company A, 10th Regiment, New Jersey Volunteers.

PREFACE.

DEAR READER:—In writing this book I do not wish to cast reflections on the people of the South, no, not even so much as to mention their names. I write this only to give you a true and full description of what I saw and experienced in the Rebel Prison Pens of the South, in the last year and the dark hours of the rebellion, for many have said "how is it that the Rebs starved our men to death and still there seems to be so many of our ex-prisoners still alive?" To answer this question in a proper form it must be done in writing, for this generation will soon pass away, and without a written history this thing will never be understood, and this is why I write. These prison pens of which I write, one was located at Andersonville, Georgia, and one at Florence. South Carolina.

CHAPTER I.

My Enlistment, Capture and Journey to Andersonville. Andersonville Stockade or Prison Pen. How It was Made. Where the Guards were Stationed. The Dead Line.

I enlisted in the Union or the United States Army on the tenth day of September, 1861, for three years, or during the war. I was captured at or near Spottsylvania, Va., on or about the fourteenth day of May, 1864. The Rebs had fell back from Spottsylvania and two or three regiments where sent out on the morning of the 14th to find where they had made their line of battle. I was among those sent out and we had not gone more than two miles before we found them in a strong position. We opened the fight and before our main lines of battle could get to us, we where charged on by the Rebs and about twelve hundred of us were killed, wounded or captured. Here it was we had both of our color bearers shot down and one of our colors or flags captured; but for the battles and fighting of that month and year, see history of the war or of the civil war in the United States. As soon as we were captured the Rebs said: "your side have lost forty thousand in the last ten days' fight." We said: "thats all right; our army has been reinforced forty thousand from the North since the fight commenced, so you see we are just about as strong now as we were the fourth of May." The Rebs said they "did not care; they had whipped all our Generals of the Army of the Potomac, and this time they would whip Grant worse than all the rest.

The Rebs took us two or three miles south of their army where we met about one thousand prisoners. We now numbered about two thousand men and several officers.

The officers were here taken away and the private soldiers were marched thirty or forty miles to a place called Danville, Va.

At Danville the Rebs took our gum blankets, knives and money; some of the men hid their knives and money so that the Rebs could not find them. I had a large buckhorn penknife which they did not get and twenty cents in money which they did not take; they would not take less than a dollar. We received from the Rebs nine hardtacks or bread and one pound of bacon or meat.

This they said would last us three days. We were now put in box cars and started South. The Rebs said "we will now show you Yanks how large our country is." It was now the seventeenth day of May, 1864.

The Rebs now took us South. We traveled in daylight and stopped off at nights. We traveled on down through Virginia, North Carolina and South Carolina on to about the center of Georgia, where we stopped at a place called Andersonville, a small station on the Georgia Central R. R. about sixty miles South-east from Macon, Ga.

The Rebs now took us off the cars and marched us about one mile, and then we stood before and in sight of Andersonville Stockade or Prison Pen. This was the twenty fifth day of May, 1864. The Rebs now divided or counted us off into detachments of thousands, hundreds and twenty-fives. The twenty-five were called a mess. Some of the men wanted to know what they were going to do with us. The Captain in charge said, "we are going to put you in that Stockade and there we are going to keep you until your Government takes you out."

It was now about six o'clock in the evening; the gate of the Stockade was opened and we were marched into the Prison, tired, hungry and disappointed.

There were about ten thousand prisoners in this Prison at this time

Andersonville Stockade or Prison Pen was a pen of about sixteen acres of land, without shelter of any kind except two pine trees that stood in the Northern part of the Prison. Those two trees were cut down on or about the first of July. Wood was so scarce in the prison we had to take the trees to do our cooking.

What little shelter we had was what the prisoners made themselves with their blankets, clothing or what ever they hapened to have when they entered the prison. The Rebs gave us nothing for shelter.

This Prison Pen was inclosed by a Stockade of pine logs sixteen feet long set close together, four feet in the ground, or twelve feet above the ground, or twelve feet high, with two gates, both gates being on one side of the prison, one gate at the upper and one at the lower end, with a drive way so that a horse and wagon could come in and drive about half-way across the prison and turn.

The Reb guard had little sheds about twenty yards apart all the way around the Stockade; these sheds where made a little higher than the Stockade so that the guards could stand in them and watch the Prisoners.

These sheds where on the outside above the stockade. On the inside all the way around was the dead line, and it was certain death for any one who dared to cross the dead line; this dead line on the inside of the Stockade or Prison Pen, was thirty feet from each side and end, and was marked by a small railing nailed on top of stakes driven in the ground and about two feet high.   This railing did not last long for the men being always short of wood, it was carried away piece at a time until it was all gone, and there was nothing left to mark this dead line.

This was very bad for the new Prisoners coming in, for those in the prison never told them about the dead line, and very often when fresh prisoners would come in they would rush over the dead line for a place to rest and some one would be sure to be killed or wounded before they could find out their mistake.

CHAPTER II.

WHERE WE GOT OUR WATER. HOW WE DUG WELLS. THE PRICE
OF WATER. OVERRUN WITH VERMIN. HOW WE FARED
FOR SHELTER. FIGHTING LICE. MAKING A
MUD SHANTY. WHO WAS RESPONSIBLE
FOR THE WAY WE WERE
TREATED.

Through the center of this Prison was a ditch of water about one foot deep and three feet wide. About one third of this ditch at one end was used for a sink. This sink was marked by a railing, but by the first of July the railing had all been used for wood to cook with. One-third of this ditch about midway was used to wash in and there could be seen hundreds of men there day and night waiting for their turn to wash themselves; I never washed in the ditch. One end of the ditch was used for drink water.

The Rebs had a cook house on the outside near the ditch, and much of the dirt from their cook house would get in the water, which made it very bad to drink. I never drank water from the ditch. At the end of the ditch inside of the dead line was a small running spring of water. The water would run out of this spring into the ditch and many of the men would reach through or under the dead line so as to get pure water, and there could be seen hundreds of men waiting for their turn to get water there, for only one or two at a time could get water in this way.

There was so much danger that I never went there for water; too near the dead line for me.

There were about sixteen wells of water in this prison. These wells were from three to thirty feet deep but they were owned by private parties. Some of these wells would have as many as a hundred owners. We had nothing to dig these wells with; we had to dig them with our knives, tin cups and tin plates. It would take us three or four weeks to dig a well and some of the men would dig for weeks and find no water. I have seen men lowered down in these wells, twenty-five or thirty feet deep, with a leather string made from or out of a shoe. Any one who was not an owner was not alowed to use this well water, without they bought it at the rate of one cent a quart.

We had no pennies in this prison, and so when we wanted to buy water we would give one teaspoonful of corn meal, or one teaspoonful of mush or a chew of tobacco about the size of half a grain of corn. I was one of the owners of a well. The well that I had a share in was fifteen feet deep and it had eighteen owners and the water was good, we used this water to drink, to cook with, and to wash ourselves with.

The owners of the wells had to watch over them day and night. On both sides of this ditch the ground was low and muddy; the mud in some places was knee deep. The men could not stay on this low land All who tried to live there would soon get sick and die. This low muddy ground contained about three acres. From this low land up to the stockade the ground was higher and it was between the dead line and the low land where the Prisoners lived. I have seen men in this low muddy ground up to their knees in mud hunting for wood; every stump and every peice of wood was gathered and used for fuel to cook with.

This low muddy ground was used by the sick men who could not reach or get to the sink or ditch In fact, many of the men were so sick that they could not walk down to the low land, and they had to dig little holes in the ground, and after using them they would cover them over, and these holes, thousand of them, would get full and by the effect of the hot sun and rain they would boil over and run down the hill. This was the cause of creating millions of maggots, and when we would lay down to sleep hundreds of these maggots would crawl over us. Some of them would crawl in our ears and in our mouths.

The Rebs gave us nothing for shelter so we had to depend on our own resources, or whatever we would happen to have when we entered the prison, and there were thousands of little shanties or tents of all description from a shelter tent to a hole in the ground. Many of the men had no shelter. They of course would soon be taken sick and die. There was a place in this prison we called the Island It was a small neck of land that was very nearly surrounded by the low muddy ground. This island was near the center of the prison. It was on this island that I and a number of my friends located. There was about six hundred prisoners on this island, and about three hundred of them were from New Jersey. The men had no change of clothing and no soap to wash with, and living in so much dirt it was no wonder that all of the men in prison became lousy. We had to take our clothes off every day and hunt and kill the lice and nits. These were what we called body lice; we did not make much account of head lice. We had to kill the lice or they would kill us. Oh, pity the sick who could not or had not strengh enough to hunt their lice. The ground or sand seemed to be full of these lice and at any time we could see them crawling on us from off the ground.

I would like here to make a statement in regard to myself: From the fourth of July until the first day of September, every day in those two months, I killed three hundred lice and nits. When I got up to this number I would stop killing until the next day.

All the clothes I had was a hat, a coat, one pair of pants, one shirt, one pair of stockings, one pair of shoes. The first night that I landed in the prison I slept out in the open air. The next morning one of the prisoners had a board which he offered to sell for two dollars; it was an inch board twelve feet long and about ten inches wide, and Phil. Hilyard, of Williamstown, N. J.; Jacob Kay, of Longacoming, N. J.; George MacIntosh of Mauch Chunk, Pa. and I, made up the two dollars and bought the board. I put in twenty cents, all the money I had. With this board we made a frame for our shanty or tent and enclosed it with mud and clay which we dug from the low muddy ground.

This shanty or tent was one foot high at the back, three feet high at the front, four feet long and four feet wide. Phil had a wool blanket that we used for an awning on the front toward the south. It was built for four, but when we got it finished only three could crawl in at a time, but it done very well to keep the hot sun off. We were raised in the North and this was so far South we suffered much by the heat. Every time it rained very much the roof of our shanty would get soft and fall in and part of the shanty would fall down, so we had the pleasure of building it up about once or twice a week. This shanty or tent of ours was called one of the best in the prison and many of the men would come and take a drawing of it when they wanted to build. Oh, pity those who had no shelter, for there were thousands of them who had nothing to keep them from the hot sun and rain. About ten feet from our tent was the low muddy ground, and about five feet from the low land was where we dug our well of water. Now before you read too far I do not wish you to blame the common people of the South. This thing was done against their wishes. The Rebellion of the South was caused by slavery —by slave holders and slave owners only, and not by the common people—slavery caused it all; and these slave owners, after they started the Rebellion, were willing to do anything wrong to carry their point and extend slavery, and this being in the last year of the war they wanted to do something to bring the United States Government to terms, and this was one of the things they tried and failed. The Rebel Leaders were in much trouble at this time and every thing they done seemed to be wrong and bad, while on the other side the United States Government seemed to do every thing that was pure, and noble, and right. And now in regard to prison life I propose to give it in detail, and to itemize as far as my memory goes so that all who read will know how this starving of prisoners was done.

CHAPTER III.

WHAT WE HAD TO EAT.   THE REGULATORS OR POLICE.   COOK-
ING OUR OWN FOOD.   FOOD CUT DOWN ONE-HALF.   MOSBY'S
RAIDERS.   DOG SOUP.   ARREST OF THE RAIDERS.
SIX HUNG.

When I was first put in this Prison Pen the men received
their food ready cooked, of which, each one of us received half
a pound of corn meal bread, and four ounces of boiled ham or bacon for one day's food.   One day in each week we received four
ounces of fresh beef.   In addition to this we received every two
days half a pint of mush, or half a pint of cooked beans, or six
tea poonfuls of molasses; so you see part of the time we received
two different kinds, and part of the time three kinds of food.

Well we went on at this rate until June the first, new prisoners coming in every day or two, until we numbered about twenty thousand, and it took so much food that the Rebs could not
cook it for us, and some times it would be near sun down before
we would receive any thing to eat.   The mush was put in large
dry good boxes; three or four of these boxes were filled with hot
mush, put on a two horse open wagon, which the Rebs would drive
into the prison.   It took several of these boxes of mush to supply
us, and some times the men would get tired waiting, and when
the loaded wagon would come in, many of the men would make a
raid on the wagon, upset the boxes and spill the mush; in this way
it would get wasted and many of the men had to go without mush
for that day.

The Rebs and the prisoners soon got tired of this, so we had two companies of regulators or police appointed. It was the duty or work of the regulators to keep the raiders from the food wagons, for which service they received double rations. The Rebs said that they could not cook our corn meal bread for us so now they gave us our corn meal raw and wood to cook all our food except the mush, beans, rice and molasses. Generally these articles were cooked before we got them, but some times we would receive them raw. We received our ration of food about in this way: Sunday we received corn meal, saltmeat and half a pint of cooked rice ; Monday, corn meal and saltmeat ; Tuesday, corn meal, saltmeat and half a pint of mush; Wednesday, corn meal and fresh beef; Thursday, corn meal, saltmeat and six teaspoonfuls of molasses ; Friday, corn meal and saltmeat ; Saturday, corn meal, saltmeat and half a pint of cooked beans, and then on Sunday, corn meal, etc.

This is, or was, about the way they tried to feed us during the nine months that I was there. We had four separate days we received no food, twice we received no food for three days at a time, about thirty days we received no meat, and we received no mush, rice, beans or molasses for forty days at a time. These days we received nothing but corn meal and meat. When we commence to get our food raw it was on or about the first of June and from that time we had to do the cooking ourselves. Each man got his food and done his own cooking. At first we received one quart of corn meal and four ounces of meat for one day's food.

This was more corn meal than many of the men could eat, for there were many sick who did not eat one pint a day; I could eat my quart every day. Each man received a piece of wood about one inch square and three feet long every day to cook with. This wood was too small to do our cooking with and as soon as it turned out we would eat our food, very often, half cooked. We went on in this way for about three weeks. The sick did not eat their full ration of food. Corn meal was plenty, we could buy it in any part of the prison for five cents a quart. I kept about four quarts on hand. Many of the men would try to keep their meal but it would get wet and sour, and corn meal could be seen all through the prison where the men had thrown it away.

The Rebs saw this and they thought that they were giving us too much to eat, so in the last week in June our food was cut down one-half. Of mush, beans, rice and molasses we got about the same, but of corn meal and meat we received but one pint of corn meal and about three ounces of meat a day. The next day after food was cut down corn meal went up to fifty cents a quart and never sold for less during my imprisonment. I never received salt from the Rebs while in Andersonville prison. I do not think that they ever gave the Prisoners any salt except what was in the meat.

The price of salt was five cents a tablespoonful or fifty cents a pint. It was now the first of July and new prisoners were coming in and we numbered about thirty thousand. At this time we were pested with a gang of our men who were called Mosby's Raiders. There seemed to be about one thousand of these men banded together, nearly all of them were known, and we could point them out wherever we would see them. These men, or raiders did not disturb many of the old prisoners but they would steal off of the new ones when they first came in, which made a great deal of trouble in the prison.

One day three Rebs came in the prison. One appeared to be a doctor who had a little pet dog with him. I saw one of the raiders slip up behind them and steal the dog. He took it to his shan-

The Author, from a daguerreotype taken three months before his capture.

ty, killed it and made it into soup. I saw that same raider that evening going through the prison selling soup. He would sing out, "here is your nice mutton soup, twenty-five cents a pint, with a piece of mutton in every pint." The doctor never knew what became of his dog. One day these raiders stole a watch. Some said they stole it from the Rebs and some said they stole it off of one of the new prisoners. I do not know which it was for when any thing happened in the prison we could hear all kind of rumors; any way there was quite a riot started on account of it.

The watch was never found but the raiders got themselves into trouble by it. The excitement was so strong that the Rebs marched in a company of their men. They then had it explained to them how we were tormented by the raiders. The captain in charge of the prison now ordered the regulators to arrest all the raiders and send them outside to him. The regulators in two days had arrested over three hundred and sent them out. They where then tried by a court-martial composed of prisoners and rebels, six of them where found guilty of murder. One of their shanties was dug out and one of the prisoners found murdered and buried therein. Then all but the six where sent back into the prison again and they were kept out until the eleventh of July.

The Captain that had charge over the prison came in and said, "we have arrested some of your men and have given them a fair trial; six of them have been found guilty of murder; we do not know what to do with those six men; they ought to be hung, but we dare not hang them for fear your government may retaliate, so we have made up our minds to send them back into the prison and let them go. You men can take them, let them go free, hang them or do what you like with them." Every thing had

been still and silent while the captain was speaking, but now a cry
went up from five thousand men, to "hang them;" "hang them."

One of the prisoners went up to the captain in charge of the
prison and said that he would hang them if the captain would give
him lumber to build a scaffold and rope to do the hanging with,
for, said he, "these raiders have killed my brother and I want to
hang them for it." The captain said he would send every thing in
that was needed.   A wagon was sent in with the lumber and soon
the men had a scaffold built with six ropes dangling on it.   Then
about three o'clock in the afternoon the six men were brought in
hand-cuffed   The captain in charge of the prison then removed
the hand-cuffs and turned the men over to the prisoners.   The
Rebs then all went out except the Quartermaster and the Priest.
These two stayed inside the prison until after the hanging.   There
was about five thousand prisoners at this time standing crowded
together near the gate.

As soon as the six men where relieved of their cuffs one of
them, the leader of the gang, made a break for liberty.   He run
hrough this crowd of five thousand men, up and down the
prison, across the low mudy ground, wen tup to his knees in mud,
fell down, crawled out of the mud, got on the up land and kept
on running until some one run up to him and caught him.   Then
they were taken to the scaffold, the ropes put around their necks,
mealsacks pulled over their heads, and soon they were dangling in
the air.   One man broke the rope but he was put up again and
hung.   They were left hanging for about one hour when a wagon
drove in and they were then cut down, loaded on the wagon and

took out. This stopped the raiding and there was no raiders now to be found. Now if a man was caught stealing he was taken to the regulators and if found guitly, he was tied to a post, received from five to twenty lashes, and then let go.

CHAPTER IV.

DRAWING RATIONS. AMOUNT OF RATIONS IN BULK AND WHAT
EACH RECEIVED. MAKING COFFEE. THE PEN ENLARGED.
MEN GETTING WILD. PLACING CANNON ON THE
STOCKADE. CLOTHING GIVING OUT.

Now in regards to drawing or dividing our rations or food.
In every detachment or thousand men there was one Reb and one
Union man appointed over them. It was the work of the Reb
to count his thousand every morning. This was done by counting the first, second, third, and so on hundred at a time. Then
the Reb would report to the Rebel Quartermaster, draw the rations
or food, and turn it over to the Union man that had charge of the
thousand. This Union man would then divide the food into ten
parts for which service he would received a double ration of food
Each hundred had one Union man appointed over them and it was
the work of this man to draw the rations for his men from the
man that had charge of the thousand. Then this man would
divide the food into four parts for which he would receive
for his work a double ration or two shares of the food; and one
Union man had charge over the mess, or twenty-five men. It was
the work of this man to draw the portion of food for the twenty
five men and divide it and for this work he received nothing. It was the rule for the man that divided the twenty-
five rations to always take the last ration; this rule caused him to
divide it very true and exact; every man seemed to get his full
share. When we received fresh beef with a bone in it the bone

would count for one ration of meat as any of the men would take it in preference to the meat. One man told me that he had boiled his beef bone forty times, always getting a little substance out of it to season his corn meal or meal cake. At one time the man that was in charge of my mess of twenty-five got sick and died. I was appointed to divide the rations, and the first day I was short of one ration of meat. Of course I had to go without meat for that day. I divided the rations for two or three weeks; I soon found that I was losing in strength so I threw up the job and some one else took it.

It was surprising to see the large amount of food it took every day to feed the prisoners, and when it was divided we would only have about half enough to eat. I have seen ten barrels of molasses carted into the prison for one day's ration and when it was divided to thirty-five thousand men it was only six teaspoonfuls to each man. It took more than five hundred bushels of corn meal every day to feed those men, each man receiving only one pint of corn meal. It took five or six thousand pounds of meat every day and all we received was about three ounces of meat a day for each man. It took twelve or fifteen cords of wood every day and when it was divided out to each man it would not make enough fire for cooking. We had many different ways of preparing our food to eat. One way we eat the mush was to put cold water on it, then shut our eyes and imagine that we were eating mush and milk. I ate my mush often in this way and then told the men that it was hard to tell water from milk. We had many ways in using molasses; some would drink it as soon as they got it, others would trade it off for four or five teaspoonfuls o meal or a little piece of meat. Hundreds of the men had nothing to put the molasses in and they would get it in the top of their caps, or in an old rag, or in their hands. These poor fellows would have to eat theirs very quickly or loose or waste it. Some of the men would trade all of their corn meal and meat for molasses; out of the molasses they would make candy, sell it and then take the money and buy something else to eat.

I always divided my ration or food into two meals; I eat one in the afternoon or evening and the other in the morning. I had a quart tin cup and a tin plate, that I cooked in; everyday I made what I called Coffee. I took four or five teaspoonfuls of corn meal, put it in the tin plate, put the plate over the fire and burnt the meal black; then I put the burnt meal in the tin cup with one pint of water and brought it to a boil. This made very good coffee and when I drank the coffee I always ate the grounds so that nothing would be lost. I would make the corn meal out in a little water into two cakes and bake them in my tin plate over the fire; some times I would cut my meat up in small pieces, mix it with the corn meal and bake it altogether; this making the cake very good and rich. The Rebs never gave me any salt while in this prison. When I received fresh beef I always made a cup of soup and put corn meal dumplings in it. I was in these prison pens nine months and was sick only one day, so I had a fair chance to see much that was going on in the prison.

And now it was July fifteenth, and new prisoners were still coming in, and the cry was, still they come. The Prison Pen had become so full of men, that the Rebs had it enlarged, and now we had about twenty-four or five acres of land in our prison.

Our food began to get short; the overplus was all used up and now what food we received would do very well for the sick to die on, but it was far to small for heathy men to live on.

Save us! oh, save us! what shall we do. New prisoners coming in every day until the number run up to fourty thousand, with about half enough to eat, and the cry was "what shall we do" or "what will we do." There was the men that had been the bravest of the Country, who had stood before the enemy in the heat of battle and fought until they were wounded or captured, but now they are so reduced and starved that their hearts sink, their strength is gone, and they are passing away for ever. There was nothing in this prison pen but famine and danger.

The men where wild with torment; they looked one another in the eyes and wept. Some swore and some cried, some went mad, many were sick, and many died. It had not rained for several days and the prison was filthy from one end to the other, death was staring every man in the face. The Rebs too got uneasy. They planted a battery of artilery on the outside at each corner of the prison and threatened to blow us all into eternity sooner than let us escape. They unlimbered their guns and commenced firing over the prison. About this time a thunder storm arose and the lighting struck in many places all about the prison, the rain decended in mighty power flooding all of the low land of the prison the water made the ground so soft that both ends of the Stockade where it crossed the low land fell down and the water rushed through carring all the filth and dirt with it.

And now it was in August and the men's clothing began to give out; some had only a pair of pants, some only a shirt, some drawers, some only had a cap, some a pair of shoes, many were barefooted, and many nearly naked. We had a mass meeting and elected three of our men to go Washington, D. C. and see if they could make some terms for us to get away.

The Rebs said they would send the three men through the lines The three men went off and that was the last we ever seen of them.   The Rebs said that they would never exchange a black man for a white one, and that was the only terms our Government would exchange on, so there would be no exchange until the war was over.

CHAPTER V.

Dying by hundreds. The sick call. Trade and Traffic.
U. S. money in circulation. Buying off the farmers. Plenty of Confederate money and
what it was worth. Our stores and
their prices.

In July and August we had about six thousand sick men in
the prison, about three thousand of whom where almost helpless
and dying. The dead averaged about one hundred a day and one
day we had two hundred and four deaths. Every day the dead
were carried out to the dead house by four of his friends. We had
a sick call every day at ten o'clock This call was at the gate
where the doctor would come in and look at the sick. I will ex-
plain this sick call: At ten o'clock a drummer boy would come
in near the gate and beat the drum, about three thousand of the
sick would then start for the gate and about three hundred would
hold out to reach there, the rest of the men would all give out before they got near the gate and they would hear, "the sick call
is over" and they had to get back to their shanties the best they
could.   There were about two thousand men that could not walk
far at a time these men would crawl out and get from five to twenty-five yards and they would hear "the sick call is over" and then
they would crawl back to their tents and holes again.   There was
about one thousand sick who could not help themselves.

A great many of these men had their friends to help them;
these too would start to answer the sick call. Each one would have

three or four friends who would pick them up and start for the gate; some of these were carried in blankets, some on sticks of wood and some on the shoulders of their friends, each party trying to rush their man in ahead of the other. Some of these would run into each other, throw down their men and fight for the right of way. Very often when the fight was over one or the other of the sick men would be dead. This surely was a sad sight. About three hundred would reach the gate, and carried up in this way, it took a long time to reach there for our motion was very slow, we had been so reduced that we could not move fast.

Of course, the new prisoners coming in could make very fast time but they too would soon have to come down to slow time. The sick are at the gate near the dead line—that is all that were able to get there—about six or seven hundred and these hope to get medicine; two doctors come in and look at them, pick out three or four and send them out to the hospital, the doctors then gives a little red root or a few pills to about fifty of the sick men, and then the doctor says that's all we can do and tell the men to come again to-morrow; then the men are taken back to their holes and shanties again disappointed and dying.

Sometimes the sick would be waiting for the doctor and word would come that he would not be in to-day, and some of the men would give up all hope and die.

There was a great deal of trade and traffic carried on in this prison and there seemed to be about forty thousand dollars in greenbacks, or United States money, in circulation. Some of the prisoners would have as low as five cents and some as high as one hundred dollars. This money was all the time in circulation, and some of it would get so black and dirty that we could scarcely tell the value of it. All of the currency or small notes less than a dollar were kept in the prison; these we used for retail trade. There was many thousand men in this prison who never had a cent of money of any kind while they were in there. I was with the number without money while in this prison. Oh pity the poor, and the sick who had no money. The Rebs allowed the farmers to sell to the prisoners but they were not allowed to enter the prison, neither were they allowed to sell for greenbacks. The prisoners that bought off these farmers had to be escorted out of the prison under guard to buy their produce, so every day there would be a few prisoners taken out to buy goods, and some of the prisoners would stand at the gate for weeks at a time waiting for their turn. Many of them never got out for it was just who happened to be the lucky one, so those that got out would buy for those that did not. The Reb farmer was not allowed to sell for greenback so the prisoners had to buy Rebel money. Some how or other there was always plenty of this Reb or Confed money in the prison and for sale by the prisoners. How this money got into the prison or how the prisoners got possession of it I do not know. We could always buy this Confed money for there seemed to be plenty of it in prison and when we wanted to buy we would just call out, "whose got Confed to sell," and in five minutes we would see some of the prisoners coming to us with their hands full of it. The greatest mystery of all was the way this Reb money was sold. We always got five dollars of Confed money for one dollar in greenbacks, and some times we could get six for one, seven for one, and I have seen the time when we could get ten for one, and very likely the next day it would be five for one.

We always judged how things where going on in the outside world by the rise and fall of this money. We always got twenty

dollars in Confed for one in gold.   The buying and selling
on the inside of the prison was all done with United States money.
The money would have soon all disappeared if it had not been for
new prisoners coming in. Some of these men would have five, ten
or twenty dollars each and in one week's time their money would
be gone.   Many of them would start little stores or shebangs
and make out to live for weeks and months.   If a man had a dollar he was called rich, but if he had no money he was called poor
I was between the two for I was part owner of a good well of water
which threw me in with both classes.   There were many stores
in this prison and they were rated from one dollar up to twenty.
The largest store was rated at one thousand dollars and was owned
by Boston Corbet.   It was called the Novelty store and this was
the only store that kept tea, sugar, coffee and such things.   I
remember going to Corbet's store one day for five cents worth of
tea for a sick friend of mine, but he would not sell it to me.   I
told him it was all the money I had and my friend was dying. He
said tea is twenty-five cents a teaspoonful and he would not sell
any less.   I never went there to buy any thing after that.   Every
thing was very high in this prison as will be seen from the fol-
lowing prices which we paid:

Wood, fifty dollars a cord.

Butter, five dollars a pound.

Eggs, five dollars a dozen.

Pork, three dollars a pound.

Cheese, two dollars a pound.

Sugar, one dollar a pound.

Rice, one dollar a quart.

Salt, fifty cents a pint, five cent a teaspoonful.

Tea and Coffee, twenty-five cents a teaspoonful.

Corn Meal, fifty cents a quart.

Sweet Potatoes raw, five dollars a bushel.

Sweet Potatoes cooked, five and ten cents each.

Bean Soup with twenty beans, five cent a plate.

Chicken Soup, twenty-five cent a pint.

Tobacco, five cents a chew.

Sour Beer, five cents a pint.

Veal and Mutton Soup, twenty-five cents a pint.

Little long Red Peppers, five cents a piece.

Molasses Candy size of common lead pencil, five cents a stick.

If a man had a barrel he started a beer saloon and his fortune was made; all he done was to throw in corn meal and water and dip out sour beer for five cents a pint. There was three of these saloons in the prison. Tin cups and kettles where one dollar for a quart one, four dollars for a four quart kettle. These tin cups and kettes where made out of old tin that the prisoners gathered up on their way to prison and there was always ready sale for all the old tin that came in; this tin was found along the railroads where wrecks had happened. There was also a shop for repairing watches and jewelry in the prison and the men that worked in it made out well. Every man was considered lucky who made enough to buy his salt and a few extra mouthfuls of food to eat. There were four or five barber shops; shaving ten cents, hair cutting ten cents.

CHAPTER VI.

WOUNDING NEGRO PRISONERS AFTER THEY WERE CAPTURED.   MY
DREAM OF HOME. PRISONERS TRYING TO ESCAPE BY TUN-
NELS.   SHELTER FOR THE SICK.   RUMOR OF
EXCHANGE. REMOVED TO FLORENCE,
S. C. STARTING A STORE.

There was four or five hundred colored prisoners in this prison and nearly all of them where lame or wounded. Their's was
a sad fate indeed, some of them said that they had been wounded
after they were captured.   All the prisoners seemed to be affected
with the scurvy; many where broke out in black spots and some
were so bad that their teeth fell out, many were so bad that they
would swell up to twice their size and the black spots would break
and burst out, and large gangrene sores would eat the flesh from
their bones, and I have often seen the bare bones through the sores
for many days before the men were dead.   Many of the men
were troubled with the diarrhœa many died from this cause.
The corn meal did not agree with them and they had no way to
cure themselves.   The men were troubled much with fever; some
would be taken and die soon, this we called the yellow fever
and some would be taken and linger long, this kind we called
the slow fever.   They where so reduced that their hip bones had
nothing on them but the thin skin and sometimes they would get
so sore that we could see the bone.   This made the men sleep in
all ways.   Most of the time in this prison I slept in a sitting
position with my knees drawn up and my head and arms resting

on my knees. I remember one day standing at the dead line near the gate, it was about the time of the sick call and I was standing there counting the dead that had been brought up to the gate that morning, seventy-eight in number, but they had not yet been carried out to the dead house, and the prison seemed to have on all of its agony when I looked up and saw six women looking over the top of the stockade, and I heard one of them remark, "I have often wondered why the Confederacy did not succeed but now I know; no nation can prosper who does a thing like this," and the women turned from the sight. While in this prison I had many dreams and I often dreampt of going home and setting at the table filled with plenty of good things to eat. I dreampt this so often that one night when I was in a dream sitting at the table with my brother and sisters and every thing seemed to be full and plenty, when I said "there is no use of my eating because this is nothing but a dream. I have dreamed this often, I believe this too is not real." "Oh no," said my sister, "this is no dream. See," said she, "take this hot cup of coffee and eat and drink for if this was a dream I could not hand you this." "Well," I said, "I will try it this time for surely this is no dream;" so we had a good time eating and drinking but when I awoke I was very much disappointed for I was a thousand miles from home. Many of the men tried to make their escape by tunnels, these tunnels where dug under ground, three or four feet deep and three or four hundred yards long. Not many of the prisoners ever made their escape in this way, the tunnel or hole only being large enough to permit one man to crawl out at a time, the Rebs would discover them before we could complete them.

And now it is the last week of August, we have had our hard est thunder storms in this month; it flooded the prison and wash.

ed off all the filth and dirt; the ground was cold and damp and the men dying off by hundreds, the days were hot but the nights were chilly and all seemed to think that we are to be kept in this prison all Winter and the men beg the Rebs to give them shelter for the sick. The Rebs sent us in two or three wagon loads of boards and we put up two sheds open in the front and closed at the back and ends, these sheds were only for the sick that was help-less which were thousands. Many of the sick men had nothing of any kind to cook with not even so much as a tin cup or a tin plate; many of the sick and well, both, were without any thing to cook with for the Rebs gave us nothing to cook in and if the men could not borrow a tin cup or plate from their friends they had to eat their food raw. It was now the first of September, the sheds where completed and the sick was being carried to them. All that could walk was called well and all that could not walk was called sick, the four in my tent was able to walk up to this time. Kay was sick from eating raw meal, Hilyard was failing fast, MacIntosh and I were in good health. In the mud hole or tent behind my tent where three men lived, all where dead. The tent on the right side of my tent where two men lived, one was dead and the other was in good health. The tent on the left side of my tent where three men lived two where dead and one in good health. This is the way things were about the first day of September, when we had a strong rumor that the prisoners where going to be exchanged. About this time Phil Hilyard said to us, "do you men ever expect to get out of this prison alive." I told him that I hoped to get out all right. He said that he was sure that he would die before he got home; he failed fast after this and at midnight on the third of September he died. Kay got so weak that he gave up all hope and said that he believed that he too would soon die. On the seventh of September the Rebs said we would be exchanged and they began to take the prisoners out of the prison. On the eighth of September we carried Kay up and put him in the sheds; he was alive when I left the prison. On the ninth of September my old friend MacIntosh got uneasy and slipped out with another detachment and left me alone. On the tenth of September my detachment or thousand was ordered out. We were taken to the railroad and put in box cars and started North. Now I was very sad indeed; my three comrades gone, my clothes ragged and torn, I did not know what to do. I soon found that the two men that had lived along side of me was in the same car with me, one of these men was Frank Beegle of the fifteenth regiment, New Jersey Vol., and the other was Orlando Gallagher of my regiment. Both of the men had a wool blanket but I had none; we had only one blanket at our tent and when Phil got sick we sold it to get him something to eat, so these two men said that I should go with them and that they would let me sleep in the middle. This was very good news indeed to me, but still I was sad to think that we had left so many behind. It is said that fourteen thousand died in Andersonville Prison Pen, but if each man had been truly counted the dead would number many more than fourteen, fifteen or even sixteen thousand. Orlando Gallagher's partner that he had at Andersonville died and left him a silver watch valued at fifty dollars and twenty-five dollars in money. I had a gold ring worth about two dollars which I had not parted with. On the fifteenth of September we landed at a place called Florence, South Carolina. Here we were taken from the cars and put in a large field and a strong guard put over us. About eight or ten thousand prisoners had now arrived here and it was two days since we had eaten our last food. I now traded off my ring for a peck of sweet potatoes, Orlando bought some meat and corn meal, Frank hunted up some pieces of wood and we soon had a good feed. The Rebs said that they did not know that we were coming and that nothing had been prepared to feed us, so that night and the next day made three days since we had food. The men began to starve and die and we commenced to carry the dead up and lay them on the ground near the guards, some of the guards would say "what's the matter with that man." We would say that man has starved to death and every one of us will starve to death if we are kept without food another day. The Rebs thought that there was some truth in this and they started out through the country and gathered up three or four wagon loads of corn cake and sweet potatoes; this was divided with the men and the next day the Rebs began to give us our corn meal and meat regular. It was at this place that I saw three men lay on the ground and cry "oh for a spoonful of meal to save my life!" and the next morning I went to see if they where still there and there the three men lay cold and stiff in death. We received about the same amount of food that we did at Andersonville. We now formed a plot to break through the guards and escape, so the prisoners rushed out and the Rebs thought that we would all escape but by the time we had run five or six hundred yards the men gave out and as we had to stop to rest the Rebs soon surrounded us and drove us back. There seemed to be plenty to eat at this place if one only had the money to buy with, and some of the men began the same old business of keeping store.

It was now the twenty-second of September, my peck of potatoes was gone and very near all of Orlando's twenty-five dollars, so Orlando said we will sell the watch and with all we get over fifty dollars we will start a store ; so Frank and I took the watch and traded it off to an old farmer who offered us three hundred dollars in Confed money or a load of sweet potatoes. We told him if he would bring us sixteen bushels of sweet potatoes we would give him the watch, so the next day, according to promise, he brought the potatoes and we gave him the watch. As soon as we received the potatoes we sold ten bushels to the prisoners for five dollars a bushel; this made fifty dollars and we gave it to Orlando, the amount he wanted for the watch. We now had six bushel of potatoes left to start business with. Everything we sold to the prisoners in the prison we sold for greenbacks or the United States money; we never dealt in Reb money unless we wanted to buy something from the Rebs, and then of course, we got five dollars of Confed money for one dollar in greenbacks. Now I was rated with the rich, and I did not have much time to look after the sick and distressed. We took three bushels of the potatoes and made them out into twenty little heaps for which we got one dollar a heap; we now had twenty dollars and three bushels of potatoes. We bought one four quart kettle for which we paid four dollars; this kettle we used to cook our potatoes in and we sold the potatoes ready cooked for five cents each for small size and ten cents each for large size, and the next thing we bought was an eight quart kettle. This kettle we used for boiling our clothes in, and we did not have any more lice to pick, for by boiling our clothes once or twice a week we could keep clear of them. Now we went on buying and selling. One day I bought twenty dozen of little long red peppers for fifty cents a dozen in Reb money and sold them for five cents each; I bought twenty pints of salt and paid fifty cents a pint in Reb money and sold it for fifty cents a pint in greenbacks so you see we bought cheap and sold dear and sold very slow, for it was very hard work to get any thing to sell. One day

we bought a goose for five dollars in Confed; we made it into soup
and sold it for twenty-five cents a pint.   Of course we would be
a long time selling these things and by the time we could sell them
and eat a little of them ourselves not much profit was left; if we
cleared our salt we were satisfied it was better than nothing.

CHAPTER VII.

THE SICK EXCHANGED.   THE REGULATORS FIX THE PRICE OF
SELLING AND MAKE THINGS WORSE THAN THEY WERE
BEFORE.   THE CONDITION OF MY CLOTHING.
·VOTING FOR PRESIDENT.

It was now the first of October and the Rebs had made an·
other pen for us and we were now put into another stockade something like the one at Andersonville, only it was in better con·
dition—it was clean.   We had plenty of wood when we first went
in and it had a nice stream of water running through it, the stream
being about six feet wide.   We had no wells in this prison, the
water was plenty and good.   One part of this prison the Rebs
staked off for a hospital and they had made a few little huts out of
the pine brush and the sick were carried and put into these little
brush huts.   Those that could walk had to shift the best they could
for no shelter was given us in this prison.   There seemed to be
about twenty thousand men in this prison and it contained about
sixteen acres of land, mud and water.

It was now about the twenty-first of October and who did I
see coming in but my old friend George MacIntosh.   He wanted
me to take him in and I was willing but Frank and Orlando
were not, so the poor old fellow had to find another partner.
Orlando and MacIntosh were from the same place.

We got word that the sick were to be exchanged which we
soon found out was realy true and George MacIntosh and Orlando
Gallagher were taken out with the sick on account of being old

men. I was glad to see them go. It was now in November and
the regulators or police said the price of selling at the stores in the
prison was entirely to high so they went through the prison and
told the store keepers how much they should charge, and they
regulated the price so low that it turned out to be one of the
worst things that ever happened in the prison, for many of these
stores only made one or two extra messes or meals a week and
now the price being cut down there was nothing in it.

Our store was one that would not pay. We had six pints of
salt and eight dozen peppers, this we divided and stoped keeping
store and in two weeks time there was nothing to buy or sell, and
we were now left to the mercy of the Rebs, and they could starve
us all to death in four or five days if they where so inclined; we
all seemed to be dissatisfied and we where all of us like a set of
hungry hogs. Now there was no laughing, no singing and not
much talking; we all lost hope and we thought our time had come;
we were now all alike; all must die the same death. The well and
sick seemed to die together; a man would be well to-day and dead
to-morrow. Surely no one could hope to ever escape alive. The
Rebs and the regulators now saw they had made a great mistake,
and they told the men to go on with their stores and sell for any
price they pleased. Some few of the stores were opened but business never come up to where it was before. Frank and I had
spent all of our money and we had nothing but peppers, salt and
one blanket, so we did not undertake to start another store.
It was now in December and the nights were very chilly and cold
and the only way that Frank and I could keep warm was by drinking hot pepper tea. In this way we could make out to keep from
perishing. I still had a pair of pants, coat and shirt, but you
could not have told what they were; I had cut the sleeves out of

The author just before he made his escape.

my coat to cover my feet. The thread in all the seams of my
clothing had given out and I had cut the sleeves out of my shirt,
to make strings to tie my pants, coat and shirt together. They
were all torn and ragged and I had hard work to make them hang
on me and still I was better off than a great many others. Some
had only a coat, some only a shirt, others a pair of pants; we were
the worst looking creatures that ever was seen. Tongue cannot tell
and pen cannot write the terrible scenes of this prison pen.

It was now the first of January and we heard that the North,
or the people of the North, had sent down some clothing to the
prisoners. I saw the Lieutenant in charge of the prison and
begged him to give me some clothes; he took me out to where the
clothes were and told me to pick out one piece, for said he:
"Each man will get one peice and then we will not have enough
to go half way around." I told him that I would take a blanket,
for I could wrap it around me and keep warm.

The wood that we used in this prison to cook with was cut by
negro slaves near the prison, and it was carried up to the gate, by
one hundred prisoners, the same ones going out every day to carry
up wood; they would go out in the morning and come in at night,
or about five o'clock in the afternoon. These men got the last
load they carried and a double ration of food every day. Frank,
about this time, got on the wood gang and now every thing was
lovely again, for all I had to do was to take care of the blankets
and every night Frank would bring in enought wood to keep us
warm.

One day he brought in an axe and we soon had enough poles
or logs and I went to work and built a tent. Frank brought in
six meal sacks and out of these we made the roof. In the end of
the tent we made a fireplace and the chimney extended two feet

above the top of the tent; in the back part we made a bunk or place
to sleep on, and Frank brought in some dry grass and we then had
a nice, soft bed to sleep on. I would trade off wood and loan our
axe and kettles enough to about double my rations, so Frank and
I were all right for the Winter. For the loan of a kettle or our
axe we would get one teaspoonfull of corn meal.   Now the
Rebs offered to take the men out if they would join their army.
About one thousand men went out hoping by this way to make
their escape; the Rebs gave these men a gray uniform kept them
out about two weeks and then sent them in the prison again telling them they were no good.

We were in this prison on election day, when Abraham
Lincoln and George B. McClellan run for President of the
United States, and the Rebs tried to get the men to vote, for they
wanted to know the feelings of the prisoners, so in the morning
when they counted us they gave the order for the McClellan
men to step to the left and the Lincoln men to the right, and
they only found one company, or one hundred, that gave
McClellan a majority; all the rest gave Lincoln a large majority.

They tried again through the day with white and black beans
but with the same result,   Some of the Rebs said they thought
the war would soon be over, but we said not until the slaves are
free then they said "the war will never end, for we will not give
our slaves to the Yankees" they did not seem to understand the
question.   We now gave up all hope of getting out of this prison
until the war was over.

We told the Rebs that we had come to free the black man,
save the country, union and flag.   They did not seem to understand what we said for they said: "You Yanks keep away from us
and we will not hurt you."

We had what we called a hospital in this prison but we did not have any doctor or medicine, and when the men would get sick so they could not help themselves they were carried to the hospital to die. This Hospital was so filthy and dirty that we all thought it was dangerous to go near it; the other part of the prison we considered in fair condition. But some of the men who had not been sick would go to sleep and never awake, this put us in great fear and we could hear some of the men saying to one another, "if I get asleep do not let me sleep too long or I might wake up in another world."

I was better off in this prison than I was at Andersonville for there I was classed with the poor, but here I was called a retired merchant; but if my friend Frank had not secured work carying up wood we surely would have died.

CHAPTER VIII.

MANY DYING AND THE REBS FURNISHING MUSIC TO CHEER THE MEN.
REMOVAL. TRYING TO ESCAPE FROM THE CARS. THE
PEOPLE OF WILMINGTON, N. C., NOT ALLOWED
TO BRING US FOOD. SOUND OF CANNON-
ADING. ESCAPE. RETURN
HOME.

In December and January the nights were cold and many men were frozen to death. I saw two men who did not have any shelter dig a hole in the ground and crawl in and try to keep warm but in the morning they where both frozen to death. I saw one man who had so many lice on him that he died; he was so weak that they killed him; there was no one to help him, for each one had all he could do to save his own life. All was famine, danger and death.

The Rebs said they did not know what to do; they thought that we would soon all die. They had their brass band to come near the prison on the outside of the Stockade and play a few tunes; they said they thought that it would cheer the men up, but it did not seem to do any good, so they soon stopped it from playing.

We counted four thousand dead carried out of this prison and there were many more we did not count. We can not tell how many died for we do not know the exact number. It was now the first of February and in my mess of twenty five men there was only three that was called well, the rest were all sick and they did not have the strength to look after their rations or food, so the three well ones had to do all the work, we had to draw the rations, divide them and carry them to the others and by the time we had the food divided and each man's wood split up so that he could use it we were very near tired out.   When men would die out of the mess, it would be filled up the next morning by other men, some times by new, some times by old prisoners.   The first week in February we received orders to be ready to move and the Rebs commenced to take the men out.   Frank and I had saved up enough corn meal to last three or four days so we baked some good hard corn meal cakes and got ready to travel.

The order came to go out at sunset.   Frank and I thought, perhaps, that the Union Army was about to capture the prison so we stayed back and would not go, so when the thousand went out we were reported missing and it was not long before we were surprised by two of the Rebs guards with fixed bayonet.   They tore down our tent and took us out at the point of the bayonet. About nine o'clock in the evening we were put in box-cars and started for North Carolina.   We were on these cars for two or three days and they did not seem to know what to do with us.   One night they run the cars on a siding and as the guards were tired out they all fell asleep.   The car door was shut and the guards were on top of the cars and we thought that we would all smother, as there were sixty-five men in our car.   Two of them were dead and several more, we did not think, could live until morning.   Some men began to cut a hole through the end of the car.   At last we got a hole large enough for a man to crawl out.

I was to be the fifth man out; two men had got out; the third was Joe Bureaugh, the fourth was Sergeant Blasdell.   These two men where from Wisconsin.   About the time the fourth man got half way out the guard fired and shot Joe through the arm. The two first men out made their escape, but Joe had to crawl back into the car. The next morning the Rebs took him and the three dead men out. I do not know how he made out for that was the last time I ever saw him.

After this we were put on and off the cars for several days, and one night about nine o'clock we stopped at a small town in North Carolina, here they told us we where all to be exchanged. The next day they took us off the cars, fed us and told us to go where we pleased. We thought sure we was to be exchanged so we did not try to run away. We got some fence rails, made a large fire and took things easy.

A few days after this we stopped at Wilmington, N. C. As soon as we stopped there we were taken from the cars and put into a field a short distance from the town; here we were kept all day without food. Many of the people came out to see us and when they saw that we were in a starving condition some of them offered to bring us food, so the Reb officers that had charge of us told them to bring us what they wanted too on the next day. So the next day about nine o'clock, in the morning about four or. five hundred men, women and children, both white and black came out with tubs, baskets and buckets, filled with good things to eat, but when they got within two or three hundred yards of us they were stopped by the Reb officers and ordered or drove back. They were not allowed to bring us a mouthfull. About this time the Rebs received some corn meal and beef, and we received our rations or food which was one pint of corn meal and four ounces of corned or salt beef. This was the last food that I ever received from them About this time there seemed to be great excitement among the Rebs.

We had heard cannon firing all day and it seemed to be getting nearer and nearer. Some of the Reb guards said it was time now to stop the war and the men ought to all throw down their guns and go home. They too seemed to fare about the same as the prisoners, for they had only received salt beef and corn meal for their food on this day, and they all seemed to be dissatisfied. Some of the boys that had come out to see us, said the Yankees will take the town to-night or to-morrow and you prisoners will all be free again. Sergeant Blasdell and I thought the time had come to make our escape, so we went out over the line without being noticed by the guard and the first house we come to was that of an old colored lady. We wanted the good old black women to show us a place to hide for the fields, woods, roads and lanes seemed to be full of Rebs, and we did not know what minute we would be arrested and taken back.

The old colored lady said that she had three of our men hid away and that she was afraid to hide any more but she said to an old colored man "here Wash, you take the two men and show them where to hide." Old "Uncle Wash" as we called him took us down into the swamp where we found three young colored men with their master's horses, trying to keep them from falling into the hands of the Rebs. Uncle Wash told us that he knew all the Rebels and all the Union men in the city of Wilmington, and he said, "take them all, black and white, and the most is for the Union."

The young colored fellows now told Uncle Wash to go back home and that they would take care of us, so these young men took us into the swamp, dug a hole, put us in it and coverd us up with leaves. "Now," they said, "do as we tell you and we will get you free." by this time another prisoner had come to us and

he too was put in the hole. About sunset two Rebel soldiers
came along with their guns and discovered us. We thought now
our time had come. They wanted to know what we were doing
there and we told them that we were three Andersonville prisoners
and that we were trying to make our escape. They said that they
lived at Wilmington and was trying to get home, and they went
on toward the city.

The young colored men now came to us and said, "we will
have to get away from here for the woods are full of Rebs," so they
took us about half a mile to another woods and then went back
and got their horses. It was now about nine o,clock in the evening and one of them said that he would take his horse and go into the city and see what was going on and get something to eat.
About eleven o'clock he came back and said the Rebs are leaving
and people thought the Yankees would take the town to-morrow.
He brought a basket, in which he had half a ham nicely cooked,
some corn bread and a pint of brandy. The colored men made
a fire and told us to help ourselves. This food was a great sur-
prise to us as we did not think of getting any thing to eat that
night, in fact, I was so anxious to get away from the Rebs that I
had almost forgotten about being hungry, but we commenced to
eat and had the basket empty before daylight next morning, the
black men eating but very little. They said it would take more
than one basket full of food to fill us up.

We could hear the Rebs falling back and leaving the town all
that night. Some times we would put out our fire until they
passed by. The next morning was the twenty-second of February.
We set around our fire and talked until nine o'clock, when one of
the colored men said that he would ride into town and see what
he could find out. About ten o'clock he came back and told us

to come out and go to the city for the Rebel soldiers had gore away and the Lincoln soldiers were marching into the town, and the Stars and Stripes were waving over the city.

We had about one mile to go and by the time we got there our number had incresed to five or six hundred men who had made their escape the day before. This surely was a day to be remember-ed. The people of the city were much excited, particularly the Slaves. They seemed to be almost crazed with joy. The colored women run up and down the streets singing and praying. They said that they had been praying for many years for the Lord to set them free, and now they could praise his name, for "Massa" Lincoln's Soldiers had come and set them free.

The white people of the town were very friendly to the escap-ed prisoners and took us to their homes, and fed us and used us well. Blasdell, myself and the other prisoner that was with us were all taken to one house, where we received the very best of treat-ment. The first they gave us was a pound of soap and ten plugs of tobacco each. It was the first soap I had had for nine months. They said "you men go down to the river and wash, and then come back here to this house and stay until you get some strength." I did not use tobacco, so on my way down to the river I sold my ten plugs to the colored Union soldiers for one dollar a plug and got from a white regiment a full suit of clothes, so now I had ten dollars in money, a good suit of clothes and a home to go to. The other two men had fared about the same as I and arriving at the river we threw off our old rags and went into swim. We took a good wash, dressed in our new clothes and went back to the house. Here we were used the very best; plenty to eat and a good bed to sleep on. We had no guide to our appetite, so eat of everything that was put on the table.

The men eat so much that some got sick and many died. In three days Blasdell and I had to take our man to the hospital; in one week I was taken to the hospital where I was sick for two weeks. I do not know how my friend Blasdell made out for I never saw him after I went to the hospital. As soon as I got well I wrote home telling them that I had made my escape and that I would soon be home. It was now the third week in March the doctor told me that I could go home in the next boat, so in a day or two I started with many others in a steamboat for home. We arrived at Annapolis, Md., where we were met by many friends and a brass band; we stayed at Annapolis for two or three weeks where many of the men were sick and died.

I now went to Trenton N. J. where on the twenty-fourth of April, 1865, I was discharged and mustered out of the United States service, where I had been for three years, seven months and fourteen days. I now returned home which was at Port Elizabeth, Cumberland County, New Jersey.

FINIS.

THE PHANTOM ARMY.

BRET HARTE.

And I saw a phantom army come,
With never a sound of fife or drum,
But keeping step to a muffled hum
    Of wailing lamentations;
The martyred heroes of Malvern Hill,
Of Gettysburg and Chancellorsville-
The men whose wasted bodies fill
    The patriot graves of the nation.

And there came the unknown dead, the men
Who died in fever-swamp and fen,
The slowly starved of prison pen;
    And marching beside the others,
Came the dusky martyrs of Pillow's fight,
With limbs enfranchised and bearing bright,
I thought—'twas the pale moonlight—
    They looked as white as their brothers.

And so all night marched the nation's dead,
With never a banner above them spread.
No sign save the bare, uncovered head
    Of their silent, grim Reviewer;
With never an arch but the vaulted sky,
With not a flower save those which lie
On distant graves, for love could buy
    No gift that was purer or truer.

So all night long moved the strange array;
So all night long till the break of day
I watched for one who had passed away
    With a reverent awe and wonder.
Till a blue cap waved in the lengthening line,
And I knew that one who was kin of mine
Had come, and I spoke—and. Lo! that sign
    Wakened me from my slumber.

INDEX.

ILLUSTRATIONS.

www.ingramcontent.com/pod-product-compliance
Lightning Source LLC
Chambersburg PA
CBHW022039080426

42733CB00007B/896